Community Helpers

Supermarket Managers

by Mary Firestone

Consultant:
Richard Turcsik
Senior Editor
Progressive Grocer

Bridgestone Books
an imprint of Capstone Press
Mankato, Minnesota

Bridgestone Books are published by Capstone Press
151 Good Counsel Drive, P.O. Box 669, Mankato, Minnesota 56002
http://www.capstone-press.com

Library of Congress Cataloging-in-Publication Data
Firestone, Mary.
    Supermarket managers/by Mary Firestone.
    p. cm.—(Community helpers)
    Includes bibliographical references and index.
    Summary: A simple introduction to the work supermarket managers do, discussing where they work, what tools they use, and how they are important to the communities they serve.
    ISBN 0-7368-1614-3 (hardcover)
    1. Supermarkets—Management—Juvenile literature. 2. Grocery trade—Management—Juvenile literature. [1. Supermarkets. 2. Grocery trade. 3. Occupations.] I. Title. II. Series: Community helpers (Mankato, Minn.)
HF5469 .F57 2003
381' .148'023—dc21   2002011106

Editorial Credits
Heather Adamson, editor; Karen Risch, product planning editor; Patrick D. Dentinger, cover production designer; Alta Schaffer, photo researcher

Photo Credits
Corbis/R.W. Jones, cover; Mark Tuschman, 12; Ariel Skelley, 4; Chuck Savage, 14; Progressive Image/Bob Rowan, 20
Index Stock Imagery/Stewart Cohen, 8
PictureQuest/Bob Llewellyn/Pictor International Ltd., 10, 16, 18
USDA/Ken Hammond, 6

Table of Contents

Supermarket Managers

Supermarket managers run supermarkets. These stores sell groceries and other items that people use every day. Managers make sure the food is fresh and the shelves are stocked.

stock
to keep shelves full by replacing sold items

What Supermarket Managers Do

Supermarket managers do many jobs in the store. They keep track of costs and manage workers. They order products from vendors. They lower prices on items that will spoil soon. Managers make sure workers remove old food from the shelves.

vendor
a person or company who sells items to a store

What Supermarket Managers Wear

Supermarket managers keep their clothes neat. They often wear suits. They sometimes wear an apron to protect their clothes. Managers often wear a nametag.

Tools Supermarket Managers Use

Supermarket managers use tools to run the store. Computers and scanners help them order and track items. Managers make schedules to keep track of workers. They figure prices with calculators.

scanner

a machine that reads and stores data

Skills Supermarket Managers Need

Supermarket managers need many skills. They must be helpful to their customers and workers. Managers must understand math. They need to know how to order and store supplies.

How Supermarket Managers Learn

Supermarket managers learn their jobs in many ways. Some go to college. Other managers learn by working different jobs in supermarkets. Managers also go to training programs and read business magazines.

Where Supermarket Managers Work

Supermarket managers work in all areas of a supermarket. They go to the deli, bakery, stock rooms, and other places. They make sure the store is clean and safe. They spend much of their time in the office. They make budgets and schedules.

budget
a plan for spending money

17

People Who Help Supermarket Managers

Supermarket managers have many workers to help them. The workers keep the floors clean and the shelves stocked. Cashiers add up customers' bills. Truck drivers haul groceries to stores. Other workers update prices and make sale tags.

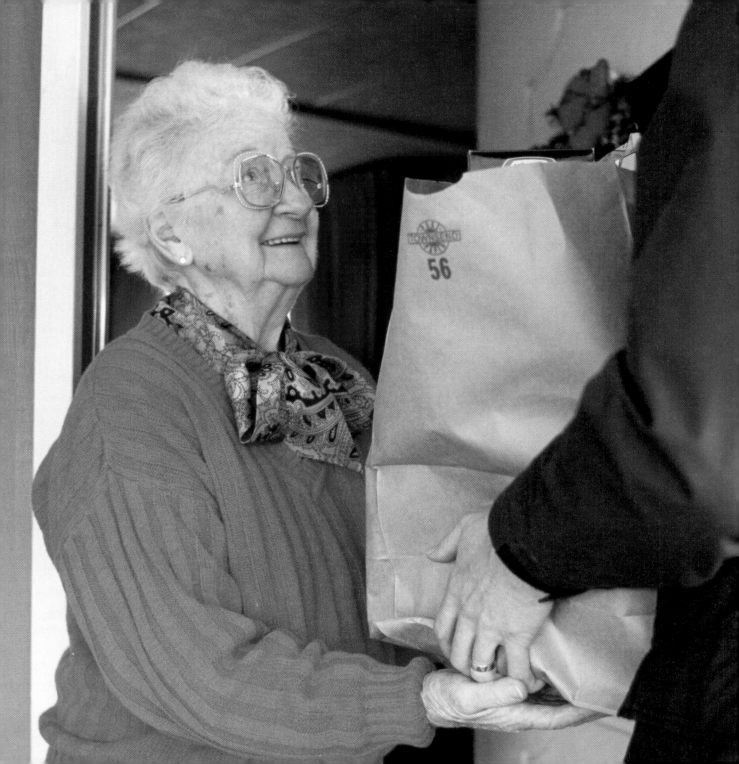

How Supermarket Managers Help Others

Supermarket managers help everyone by selling food that is safe and fresh. They have groceries delivered to people who cannot drive. Managers sometimes have their stores support sports teams or give food to people in need.

Hands On: How Much Is Your Food?

Supermarket managers decide which food items to sell in their stores. Different companies make the same items. You can think like a manager when you compare prices and decide which company's brand is best.

What You Need

Pen or pencils
Paper
An adult to help

What You Do

1. Write a list of two or three of your favorite foods. It can be snack foods, treats, or dinners.
2. Have an adult take you to the supermarket. Bring your list.
3. Find the items from your list and write down the prices.
4. Look around the shelf for a different brand of the same item. Write down the price of that item as well.

Think about trying a new brand. Does this brand cost more than the other brands? Supermarket managers must choose what brands to sell in their stores. They try to give their customers the best choices and the best prices.

Words to Know

budget (BUHJ-it)—a plan for spending money

cashier (kash-YEER)—a person who accepts money from customers for items purchased

college (KOL-ij)—a place where students study after high school

customer (KUHSS-tuh-mur)—a person who buys goods or services

groceries (GROH-sur-ees)—food and household items like soap and napkins

schedule (SKEJ-ul)—a plan for doing activities at certain times

vendor (VEHN-der)—a person or company who sells items to a store

Read More

Krull, Kathleen. *Supermarket.* New York: Holiday House, 2001.

Schaefer, Lola M. *Supermarket.* Who Works Here? Chicago: Heinemann Library, 2000.

Internet Sites

Track down many sites about supermarket managers. Visit the FACT HOUND at *http://www.facthound.com*

IT IS EASY! IT IS FUN!
1) Go to *http://www.facthound.com*
2) Type in: 0736816143
3) Click on "FETCH IT" and FACT HOUND will find several links hand-picked by our editors.

Relax and let our pal FACT HOUND do the research for you!

Index

j381
FIR

Firestone, Mary.

Supermarket
managers.

$18.60   02/24/2003

DATE